DISCORD

Its Causes and Remedy

By

Lourdes Lewin

Discord: Its Causes and Remedy
ISBN: 979-8-9878522-3-1

Most scriptures are taken from the King James Version of the Bible, except otherwise stated.

This book may be ordered by contacting
the author, Lourdes Lewin
P.O. Box 360047
Brooklyn, NY 11236
or by emailing: eternalcreationsjcml@yahoo.com

Cover Design by Cerus Scott Davis
For Alll-That!!! Graphic Design

~~~~~~~~~~~~~

Dedication

~~~~~~~~~~~~~

This book is dedicated to

> *Every person who has*
> *been affected and*
> *afflicted by discord*

Whenever we are tempted by sin, God always makes a way of escape.

1 Corinthians 10:13

There hath no temptation taken you but such as is common to man: but God is faithful, who will not suffer you to be tempted above that ye are able; but will with the temptation also make a way to escape, that ye may be able to bear it.

The greatest and most important thing for you to know is that whenever you acknowledge your failure, it allows God to forgive and restore you.

PREFACE

This book came about as a result of a conversation I had with God my Father. I questioned Him regarding my predisposition to make new friends and then lose them because something went off track.

His response to me was, "it all started in the Garden of Eden." This prompted me to review what happened in the Garden, and I discovered several factors which influenced mankind and brought about a separation between God and man, in the same way it happens today between man and man.

In this book I have explored these influences, and shown how each one of them can cause a disruption in friendships, relationships and fellowship among the children of God.

May God speak to your heart as you read, and bring understanding and comfort, as He did mine.

Lourdes Lewin

INTRODUCTION

What is Discord?

Merriam-Webster's dictionary describes it this way: *discord implies an intrinsic or essential lack of harmony producing quarrelling, factiousness, or antagonism.*

Let us look at what the Bible says about discord

Proverbs 6:16-19:
16 These six things doth the Lord hate: yea, seven are an abomination unto him:
17 A proud look, a lying tongue, and hands that shed innocent blood.
18 A heart that deviseth wicked imaginations, feet that be swift in running to mischief,
19 A false witness that speaketh lies, and he that soweth discord among brethren.

What does it mean to sow discord? That happens when a person goes around whispering lies against another, creating distrust and strife. The character of such person is evil. Often when discord is sown, the individual 'throws the stone and hides the hand.' The sower of discord is naughty and wicked, without concern for the damage caused by his/her acts.

Proverbs 6:12-14
12. A naughty person, a wicked man, walketh with a froward mouth.

13 He winketh with his eyes, he speaketh with his feet, he teacheth with his fingers;
14 Frowardness is in his heart, he deviseth mischief continually; he soweth discord.
15 Therefore shall his calamity come suddenly; suddenly shall he be broken without remedy.

What are the effects of sowing discord? Discord causes disappointment in the victim's heart, and the emotional impact can be devastating. The Word quoted above tells us that He who sows discord brings about sudden calamity; "suddenly he shall be broken without remedy."

A person who sows discord is regarded as a wicked man who delights in bringing dissention. He is a troublemaker who cannot wait to cause more problems or to get into more mischief. Let us not fall into this category.

Chapter One

THE POWER OF OUR WORDS

It is imperative that Believers know the principles of the Word of God.

We often come against each other without being fully aware that God defends His people. We treat each other without esteem, acting negatively towards one another. We really do not understand what we do.

The unregenerated person is excusable, because he or she does not understand that when they come against a Believer, God is our defense; He fights for us.

The Talebearer

Traits of a talebearer: A talebearer stirs up strife, causes confusion, sows discord, divides and severs relationships. The heart of such person is filled with hatred, deceit, jealousy and much more.

- ❖ A talebearer conceals his business, but discloses the secrets of others.
- ❖ A talebearer is not a trustworthy person; he is highly critical
- ❖ A talebearer is an insecure person who becomes an instrument of control to keep on top of what is going on
- ❖ A talebearer is a hypocrite

It is important to note that the talebearer is unaware of the fact that he is being used by the enemy. He does not realize that he causes wounds in the lives of the people he encounters.

When the talebearer sows discord in others' lives, it is done in secret, but God sees in secret and knows the pain.

Proverbs 18:8
The words of a talebearer are as wounds, and they go down into the innermost parts of the belly.

A spiritual wound is far more damaging that a physical wound. The pain of a physical wound will eventually be forgotten after it heals – only scars remain to show that there was a wound. On the other hand, a spiritual wound goes deep into the heart and it takes a longer time to heal.

A talebearer is not just a gossiper, but a slanderer; actively seeking to destroy another's reputation. He revealeth secrets; but he that is of a faithful spirit conceals the matters.

Allow me to share an experience from my life. During the mid 70's I encountered an incident with tale bearing, strife and discord.

I was working for a prestigious firm in my country of Panama. There were several of us in the office and we got along very well, until one day one of my co-workers decided to sow discord among us. She communicated a lie to another young lady who was close to me saying that I told someone who didn't work with us (someone on the outside) something about her. The situation got very intense. I felt wrapped up and trapped, having an impression that there was no way out. I noticed that no one was communicating with me on that particular day. There was a morbid silence in the entire office. I asked around until one of them informed me of the source of this discord and identified the strife maker.

I waited until the end of the work day and inquired concerning the whereabouts of the sower of this discord. Believe me! The feeling to expose this culprit was intense! I could hardly wait to confront this person. I assured the other employees that I was going to solve this problem and clear my name from such accusation.

I was informed that she was in the movie theatre with her husband; and as you can imagine my next move was to go straight way into that theatre and summon her outside. Her husband was puzzled, wondering what was going on, while she kept saying to him "these are my friends who came to see me." I exclaimed "liar!" At this point everyone walking by and those who were in the theatre came out to witness the brawl.

With all my co-workers standing around looking and listening to the confrontation, she began to stutter. I informed her of the lie she had spoken about me, but I did not tell her who had said what. She immediately tried to make a liar out of the other person. It became really ugly. Her husband was very angry at her for her malicious, diabolic act. Everyone felt that he was going to handle her when they got home. A gossiper and sower of discord *must* be exposed!

Some persons invent lies to incriminate and belittle others. They gather information to take it back to others. This is the trait of a gossiper. What does the Word say about spying/eavesdropping?

Eccl. 7:21-23 NLT

Don't evesdrop on others—you may hear your servant curse you. For you know how often you yourself have cursed others. I have always tried my best to let wisdom guide my thoughts and actions.

These are the rules for Kingdom living. We must do to others the very same thing that we want others to do unto us. To be kind, trustworthy, loving and genuine does not diminish us in any way.

The agenda of a nosy and eavesdropping person is to destroy the character of the innocent. It is to cause division and malice between people.

Proverbs 20:19
He that goeth about as a talebearer revealeth secrets: therefore meddle not with him that flattereth with his lips.

While I am not condoning the act of gossiping and talebearing, I encourage you, my readers, if gossiping or eavesdropping is one of your weaknesses, make sure to

4

listen to what I have written here, so you can avoid twisting truth and spreading lies.

Gossiper vs. Talebearer

Talebearing is distasteful. It is a trust breaker. Talebearing destroys families, friendships and other relationships. There are consequences for bad behaviors. It is profitable to do well instead of evil.

> *The perverseness of transgressors shall destroy them.*

The gossiper is one who enjoys talking about someone else's private business, and the talebearer spreads it without regard.

Gossip is like a fire that needs the constant consumption of wood to keep it alive. A gossiper uses droplets of poison to keep the talebearer motivated to run and tell stories. It is an abomination to the Lord, because it causes contention, discord and possibly even death.

If this type of behavior exists among Believers, it is equivalent to persecuting the Lord Himself.

The Power of the Tongue

Proverbs 18:21
> *Death and life are in the power of the tongue: and they that love it shall eat the fruit thereof.*

Are you a builder or a destroyer? Which one are you? Choose to be a builder. Use your words to encourage and build up others.

Ephesians 4:29
Let no corrupt communication proceed out of your mouth, but that which is good to the use of edifying, that it may minister grace unto the hearers.

Worship and praise the Lord with your mouth; bless and encourage others with your words. Encourage others and build them up with your mouth. Here is what the Bible says about gossip:

Proverbs 17:4
A wicked doer giveth heed to false lips; and a liar giveth ear to a naughty tongue.

Gossipers and tale bearers are persons of very low character who demonstrate that, not only do they not care for others, but they do not care about themselves. It is written that we must love our neighbor as yourself.

Jealousy is a *root,* and it is one of the major reasons a person gossips about another. Gossipers display low self-esteem; they seek to cast shadows upon another in an effort to elevate themselves.

Leviticus 19:16

Thou shall not go up and down as a talebearer among thy people: neither shalt thou stand against the blood of thy neighbor: I am the Lord.

Gossip can be deadly. Tale bearing and spreading lies can be equally as deadly. The question then is, how do we eliminate this deadly disease?

James 4:5-11 - New International Version

Or do you think Scripture says without reason that he jealously longs for the spirit he has caused to dwell in us. But he gives us more grace. That is why Scripture says: "God opposes the proud but shows favor to the humble." Submit yourselves, then, to God. Resist the devil, and he will flee from you. Come near to God and he will come near to you. Wash your hands, you sinners, and purify your hearts, you double-minded. Grieve, mourn and wail. Change your laughter to mourning and your joy to gloom. Humble yourselves before the Lord, and he will lift you up. Brothers and sisters, do not slander one another. Anyone who speaks against a brother or sister or judges them speaks against the law and judges it. When you judge the law, you are not keeping it, but sitting in judgment on it.

Proverbs 26:18-22

Like a maniac shooting flaming arrows of death is one who deceives their neighbor and says, "I was only joking!" Without wood a fire goes out; without a gossip a quarrel dies down. As charcoal to embers and as wood to fire, so is a quarrelsome person for kindling strife. The words of a gossip are like choice morsels; they go down to the inmost parts.

Proverbs also speaks about the mouth.

Proverbs 4:24
Put away from thee a froward mouth, and perverse lips put far from thee.

The Amplified version reads:
Put away from you false and dishonest speech, and willful and contrary talk put far from you.

We can appreciate this counsel given by Solomon to his son to put away froward and crooked speech and corrupt and obscene talk. Jesus also spoke about the abundance of the heart:

Luke 6:45:
A good man out of the good treasure of his heart bringeth forth that which is good; and an evil man out of the evil treasure of his heart bringeth forth that which is evil: for of the abundance of the heart his mouth speaketh.

Let us take a closer look at Proverbs 4:24: "Put away from thee a froward mouth, and perverse lips put far from thee."

Definition of forwardness:
> willfully contrary; not easily managed. obstinate, willful, wayward, unmanageable difficult.

To be froward means to be habitually disposed to disobedience and opposition.

Solomon's warning to his son is sound because it is vital that we adhere to this principle in our lives. When we do this, it is called progressive sanctification – a process in which God cleanses and burns out the dross and gives us instructions to avoid those things which will hinder us.

Matthew 12:35
> *A good man out of the good treasure of the heart bringeth forth good things: and an evil man out of the evil treasure bringeth forth evil things.*

Matthew 12:35 shows us a contrast between a good man and an evil man. A good man out of the good treasure of the heart bringeth forth good things: What does it mean by the treasure of the heart? It is the abundance of precious and valuable fruit -- a wealth of goodness. On the other hand, the evil man, out of the evil treasure of his heart bringeth forth evil things. Frowardness is the accumulation of bad and evil thoughts which are deposited in the heart. When frowardness is present in the heart, it divises mischief continually.

In the previous verse, Matthew 12:34, Jesus addressed a group of Pharisees and religious leaders who practiced legalism. They came to Jesus with accusations, but Jesus called them out! He said *"O generation of vipers; how can you being evil, speak good things? For out of the abundance of the heart the mouth speaketh."* My friends! Whenever evil is present in the heart it comes out when that individual opens his mouth. If good is in the heart, out of its treasure comes forth good fruit.

Here is a simple analogy which illustrates the point. When we hear the word treasure, we may think of a treasure chest similar to those often seen in pirate movies. The treasure chest is full of sparkly precious stones, gems, trinkets of gold and of silver and other rare keepsakes. In contrast, what would you find in an evil chest? Perhaps a chest full of snakes, bats, tarot cards, skulls, skeleton bones; all sorts of spiders and their webs; and a concubine trapped in a genie lamp. If you were to keep searching you would find a great assortment of dark, evil creatures.

We must endeavor to store good things in our chest, such as precious principles and great spiritual gifts so that whenever we open our mouth, from the abundance of the heart richness will flow forth to edify others. We must avoid corrupt communications which leads to an evil heart, harboring strife, discord, hypocrisy and other negative things. These are of no eternal value.

From a good chest comes love, joy, understanding, peace, meekness -- just like a beautifully-cut diamond or a rare black pearl; a block of gold, rubies, jasper, onyx or other beautiful gems.

Chapter Two

THE BEGINNING

When Adam and Eve were in the Garden of Eden, they were contented to meet with God every day. God gave them everything they needed. He would meet with them in the cool of the day and they enjoyed fellowshipping with Him, and He with them.

Then what happened? Satan, the serpent, approached Eve with deception, creating doubt in her mind against God, ultimately resulting in discord, contention and strife.

Discord: disagreement between two people. hostility
Contention: heated disagreement, dispute, argument, conflict, and disharmony.
Strife: angry or bitter disagreement over important fundamental issues.

The tools Satan used in the Garden: discord, contention, *disobedience*, strife and deception, were tools used to challenge the authority of God as well as His position as Creator and Father.

Satan negated every truth God had spoken to them, including the warning that would have prevented their spiritual death.

He uses the same tactics in the Body of Christ today to discredit the divine character of God, and he does this by attacking the integrity of His Word. One of His tactics is

11

distraction — preventing someone from giving full attention to something else. He uses distraction to take our eyes off God and place them instead on his lies. Unfortunately, many children of God fall into his trap.

His Tools

Disobedience is failure or refusal to obey rules or someone in authority.

Deception: the action of deceiving someone; to trick or to lie.

Eve unwittingly fell into the trap Satan set, thereby losing all the benefits she previously enjoyed. She and ultimately Adam gave up peace of mind – not having to stress over their daily meal, their warmth, their clothing – all the basic necessities of life.

Instead, they received in its place – shame, hunger, nakedness and hard labor. Not only was a curse placed on them, but the curse affected every living creature – including the serpent which was doomed to crawl on its belly for the rest of its life.

Genesis 3:14: *"And the Lord God said unto the serpent, Because thou hast done this, thou art cursed above all cattle, and above every beasts of the field; upon thy belly shalt thou go, and dust shalt thou eat all the days of thy life."*

Eve's special curse related to childbirth. Whereas she had never known pain, she was now forced to endure a painful childbirth. This, as you know, has travelled down through the years to this present time.

Genesis 3:16, *"and unto the woman he said, I will greatly multiply your sorrow and thy conception; in sorrow thou shalt bring forth children; and thy desire shall be to thy husband, and he shall rule over thee."* All women will bear children in pain.

Adam's special curse related to hard labor. While in the Garden he only had to reach out his hand and pick fresh fruit and vegetables for his daily meals, now having been banished from the Garden, he had to dig, plant, water and reap before he could eat.

In addition to that, he had enjoyed a privileged relationship with all the animals – naming them, and living in harmony with them – but now Adam lost his authority and animals became an enemy which needed to be killed for clothing and food.

As God's children, we are in a similar situation to Adam and Eve in the Garden. We must recognize Satan as our enemy and not succumb to his deceptive ways. What do we stand to lose if we disobey the command of God to walk in His way? Well, we lose our benefits. What are those benefits?

Preservation: Even as God prepared everything for His first children, He has again prepared everything for us because of the coming of Jesus Christ. Everything we need is preserved in Christ.

13

Provision: Because of Jesus' death on the Cross, God has allowed us to ask for what we need when we need it, and expect to receive it.

1 John 5:14,15
> *And this is the confidence that we have in him, that, if we ask any thing according to his will, he heareth us:*
> *And if we know that he hear us, whatsoever we ask, we know that we have the petitions that we desired of him.*

Matthew 7:7 – New International Version
> *Ask and it will be given to you; seek and you will find; knock and the door will be opened to you.*

Protection: God promised that He will bless our going out and our coming in, so we do not have to fear and worry about being protected.

Psalm 121:8
> *The Lord shall preserve thy going out and thy coming in from this time forth and even forevermore.*

Peace: In relying on God to take care of us, our minds can be at rest. We do not need to become stressed out when we do not see the answer right in front our eyes, we have the confidence that God knows what we have need of before we even ask.

Philippians 4:19

But my God shall supply all your need according to his riches in glory by Christ Jesus.

All these benefits and more are included in the package of salvation, and if we choose not to accept the package, we forfeit our spiritual life.

Satan's Plan

Satan's plan is to deceive the elect of God – His children.

Why does he plan to do this? First of all, we must look back a little further even before the Garden of Eden, and recognize that Satan has a vendetta against God.

Before Satan roamed the earth, he was a highly respected angelic being in heaven. He had the privilege of being in the presence of God Almighty and leading the worship of God day and night.

He was not contented to do this, however, he wanted more. He wanted to receive the same adoration and worship that God did, and just that thought alone was enough to get him expelled out of heaven.

He lost his beauty, his place of prominence, and his authority because of jealousy, greed, pride and insanity. I say insanity because: what was he thinking? Did he really think that he could overthrow the Creator of the universe and his Creator?

Jealousy: the state or feeling of being jealous. To be jealous is the feeling of showing envy of someone or their achievements and advantages.

Greed: an intense and selfish desire for something, especially wealth, power or food.

Pride: a feeling of deep pleasure or satisfaction derived from one's own achievements. To be especially proud of (a particular quality or skill).

Satan's talents, beauty and musical abilities had been given him *by* God. He was music himself. There was no one like him in the area of making worship music. It must have been a momentary loss of sanity to desire to be like God Himself.

But that's all it took. Because of his pride and jealously God threw him out of heaven and he has not forgotten it. He seeks now to take revenge by getting the worship he sought from the people for whom Christ died.

He knows that worship belongs to God alone, and therefore he uses his jealousy to discourage the children of God from worshipping Him. Knowing this, however, as God's elect and precious children, we must become more intimate with our Heavenly Father through our worship, establishing a strong relationship and friendship with Him.

God's Plan for Mankind

Jeremiah 29:11
> *For I know the thoughts that I think toward you, saith the LORD, thoughts of peace, and not of evil, to give you an expected end.*

God's plan for mankind is that we be fruitful, multiply and replenish the earth.

Genesis 1:28
> *And God blessed them, and God said unto them, be fruitful, and multiply, and replenish the earth, and subdue it: and have dominion over the fish of the sea, and over the fowl of the air, and over every living thing that moveth upon the earth.*

God has provided a way of escape from the Adamic curse through the finished work of Jesus on the cross. By the shedding of His blood, we receive salvation by grace through the word of faith.

The Power of Redemption

Jesus sacrificed His life on Calvary for our sake. He has redeemed us from the curse of the law. The law was full of rules, dictatorship, works and penalties. The law is based on performance, and man's effort as outward demonstration of the works; but salvation through Jesus Christ is given to mankind by grace through faith in what He did on the cross. In reality we don't have to work for this salvation, because it is freely given. All we have to do is accept.

Jesus has redeemed us from the curse of the Law by becoming a curse for us—

> *for it is written, Curse is everyone who is hanged on a tree that the blessing of Abraham might come on the Gentiles through Jesus Christ, that we might receive the promise of the Spirit through faith.*
> *(Galatians 3:13, 14)*

The Law could not declare us righteous; it was ineffective, because it brings a curse instead of a blessing. Therefore, Jesus' willing sufferings and crucifixion for mankind ended that curse which the human race was under. He is the fulfillment of the Law.

The Promise of Salvation

Mankind needed salvation, therefore God through grace provided that salvation to everyone who believes the Gospel of Jesus the Messiah! Salvation is a gift from God. In Ephesians 2:8 we see it; "*for by grace you have been saved through faith, and that not of yourselves; it is the gift of God.*" At that moment He makes us righteous (in right standing) justified, accepted and all penalty of sin washed away by the blood of Jesus. He declares us no longer guilty of the Adamic curse; no longer guilty of eternal death. No longer alienated or separated from God. It is a legal Act of God. This declaration of justification is also the act of sanctification. Why sanctification?

The Process of Sanctification

Sanctification is separation *to* God. To be set apart to God so His purpose and plans may be accomplished.

Whenever an individual gets saved, God already has a plan in motion. He has a divine process for the believer to become more like Him, to be transformed into His image.

God daily purges, purifies (burns out the garbage) and teaches us to yield to holy living this is called progressive sanctification. This process is a preparation for glorification which is the presentation of us before God, in which He removes all spiritual defects of us the Redeemed.

Chapter Three

THE STEADFAST LOVE OF GOD

God's character is LOVE!

We do not need to earn His love, because He loves us (mankind) from the beginning of time…John 3:16 states: *"For God so loved the world, that He gave his only begotten Son, that whosoever believeth in him should not perish, but have everlasting life."*

Jesus carried the weight of the world upon Himself. There is no valley or place too deep for His blood to reach, no mountain too enormous in your life that His blood cannot reach. God knows everything about us. Psalm 139:1-10 illustrates that He is omnipresent (present everywhere). I encourage you to read the complete chapter.

God has demonstrated His love to the world. It is the love we must have for each other. The new commandment Jesus gave—

John 13:34-35 AMP
> *I am giving you a new commandment, that you love one another. Just as I have loved you, so you too are to love one another. By this everyone will know that you are My disciples, if you have love and unselfish concern for one another.*

His love for mankind was demonstrated in our redemption. He loved the world so much that while we were yet sinners, He died for us ALL, despite our messed-up state. He loved us, and has a prepared plan for us.

I will leave this question with you! If the world sees no love amongst God's people, would they come? Would they believe?

God's love is perfect, unconditional, limitless, patient, pure, and trustworthy. You can stand secure in His love.

John 15:13 – Amplified version
No one has greater love [nor stronger commitment] than to lay down his own life for his friends.

No better friend!!

Romans 5:8
But God clearly shows and proves His own love for us, by the fact that while we were still sinners, Christ died for us.

There are people who do not know that God loves them and are literally afraid of God, so much so, that they will not come to Him.

An Example from my Ministry

Some time ago I was ministering on the train in New York, and I encountered a gentleman who refused to accept the Word I was sharing with him, because he was very afraid of God. He was shaking with paranoia. There was no pretense about his fear. I assured him that he should not be afraid, because God is love. He responded "I cannot do it now." and ran away.

It is so sad, because there are many individuals in the world who, because of hard circumstances they have faced in life, believe that God has forgotten or abandoned them, or that there is no God, and they are tired and hurt.

If this is speaking to you right now, know beyond doubt that God loves and cares for you. He wants you back. Come to Him.

Friendship with Jesus

When we come back to God, Jesus becomes our friend and older brother. He is our example, and He says to us: *"I no longer call you servants, but friends, because the servant does not always know what his master is doing, but I call you friends."* John 15:15

Becoming intimate with Jesus is the greatest experience any one could ever dream or imagine. He is a faithful friend. We can have regular conversations with Him.

Proverbs 18:24 NLT states: *There are "friends" who destroy each other, but a real friend sticks closer than a brother.*

Jesus will never humiliate, betray or abandon you. Even when things seem bad, He understands, cares and forgives. He promises never to leave or forsake us. God's promises are sure; you can depend upon them.

Hebrews 13:5 (AMPV)
Let your character [your moral essence, your inner nature] be free from the love of money [shun greed—be financially ethical], being content with what you have; for He has said, "I will never [under any circumstances] desert you [nor give you up nor leave you without support, nor will I in any degree leave you helpless], nor will I forsake or let you down or relax My hold on you [assuredly not]!"

Whenever a person professes Jesus Christ as Lord and Savior, immediately provision is made. But we must trust that He will provide even when we do not know how. Trust and dependency are important.

Deuteronomy 31:6 (KJV)
Be strong and of a good courage, fear not, nor be afraid of them: for the LORD thy God, he it is that doth go with thee; he will not fail thee, nor forsake thee.

In this passage God told Moses to speak to the Israelites, letting them know that He was of age (120 years), and could no longer go out and come in, and should not go over the Jordan. He assured them that God will go before them and fight for them and destroy nations before their faces. Joshua was assigned by God to lead them. So Moses called Joshua in the presence of the Israelites and said, *"be strong and of good courage: for thou must go with people unto the land which the LORD hath sworn unto their fathers to give them; and thou shalt cause them to inherit it. God is our defender."*

The Lord has proven to defend His children on numerous occasions. He is our helper against our enemies.

Ecclesiastes 51:2
For thou art my defender and helper, and has preserved my body from destruction, and from the snare of the slanderous tongue, and from the lips that forge lies, and has been mine helper against mine adversaries:"

Intimacy with God

Jesus is the true vine, we are the branches. The believer must remain in Him, because without Him we cannot bear fruits.

John 15:4-6
Abide in Me, and I in you. As the branch cannot bear fruit of itself unless it abides in the vine, neither can you, unless you abide in Me.
I am the vine, you are the branches. He who abides in Me, and I in him, bears much fruit; for without Me you can do nothing.

If anyone does not abide in Me, he is cast out as a branch and is withered; and they gather them and throw them into the fire, and they are burned.

Quiet Times

Spending quality quiet times with the Lord is essential for intimacy with God. It establishes our spiritual foundation to make us victorious in life.

We need the Word of God; we cannot live without it. We need to hear from Him concerning our everyday situations.

Matthew 4:4
"Man shall not live by bread alone, but by every word that proceedeth out of the mouth of God"

In quiet times we are able to reflect on His goodness and to hear instructions on the path He wants us to take.

Chapter Four

THE REMEDY FOR DISCORD

First step: Repent — be sorry for your wrong doings. God is able to forgive. *1 John 1:9 "If we confess our sins, He is faithful and just to forgive us our sins and purify us from all unrighteousness."*

Second step: Guard your heart. Proverbs 4:23 states: *"Keep thy heart with all diligence; for out of it are the issues of life."*

Our heart is likened to a flower pot. If we get offended, it goes to the heart; if we are sad, it registers in the heart; if we are happy, our heart gets happy; if we are angry it is deposited in the heart. All these emotions and more are in the heart. Like the flower pot or garden, if seeds of different kinds are tossed in, could you imagine what would happen? The result would be a flower pot or a garden with various kinds of fruit trees.

People often say, "The devil made me do it!" Actually, he just drops a suggestion in one's mind; but because mankind harbors malice, bitterness, strife and unforgiveness in the heart, it makes it easier to launch out in anger and act out of character.

We must be mindful not to harbor negative thoughts, because after a time the heart becomes toxic. It is like poison to your system.

Jeremiah 17: 9, 10

The heart is deceitful above all things, and desperately wicked: who can know it?
I the Lord search the heart, I try the reins, even to give every man according to his ways and according to the fruit of his doings.

Ask the Lord to cleanse your heart

Psalm 51:10

Create in me a clean heart, O God; and renew a right spirit within me. God is willing, waiting and able to cleanse your heart and renew a right spirit in you. Just ask.

Third Step: Guard your mouth. Let your meditation and your words be lined up with God.

Psalm 19:14

Let the words of my mouth and the meditation of my heart be acceptable in Your sight, O Lord, my strength and my Redeemer.

Psalm 141:3

Set a watch, O Lord, before my mouth; keep the door of my lips

Fourth Step: eliminate toxic relationships from your life. Here is what the Word says about the danger of bad company. 1 Corinthians 15:33, KJV "*Be not deceived: evil communications corrupt good manners.*" This means that

27

bad company causes a good person's good morals to become tainted, and causes that person to stray from the principles of the Word of God.

Fifth Step. Walk in Love. Love is the remedy for all things.

1 Corinthians 13:4-8

> *Charity suffereth long, and is kind; charity envieth not; charity vaunteth not itself, is not puffed up,*
> *Doth not behave itself unseemly, seeketh not her own, is not easily provoked, thinketh no evil;*
> *Rejoiceth not in iniquity, but rejoiceth in the truth;*
> *Beareth all things, believeth all things, hopeth all things, endureth all things.*
> *Charity never faileth: but whether there be prophecies, they shall fail; whether there be tongues, they shall cease; whether there be knowledge, it shall vanish away.*

Colossians 3:12-24

> *Since God chose you to be the holy people He loves, you must clothe yourselves with tenderhearted mercy, kindness, humility, gentleness, and patience.*
> *Make allowance for each other's faults, and forgive anyone who offends you. Remember, the Lord forgave you, so you must forgive others.*
> *Above all, clothe yourselves with love, which binds us all together in perfect harmony.*
>
> *LOVE binds us together and brings everything in harmony (in one accord). It is pleasant and good when*

brethren dwell together in harmony and love, because it changes the atmosphere around us,

Let us be mindful of the Godhead (God the Father, God the Son Jesus and God the Holy Spirit) they are distinct in their function, yet in harmony with each other. We must have the same mind.

As believers we must endeavor to keep the unity of the Spirit in the bond of peace.

Romans 15:5-7 reads:

May the God who gives endurance and encouragement give you the same attitude of mind toward each other that Christ Jesus had,
so that with one mind and one voice you may glorify the God and Father of our Lord Jesus Christ.
Accept one another, then. Just as Christ accepted you, in order to bring praise to God.

CONCLUSION

Love unites — discord divides! We are Ambassadors of Christ with the Word of Reconciliation. We, the Believers, are called the "*Repairers of the Breach*" of the divide between God and the unsaved (those who need Jesus in these perilous times).

Unity in the Spirit begins in the heart. When we allow God to fix our heart then we will be able to be effective in

29

repairing the breaches in the lives of those who need deliverance. *We must live love.*

The hour is late! Jesus is coming soon! Are we ready?

www.ingramcontent.com/pod-product-compliance
Lightning Source LLC
Chambersburg PA
CBHW070258290326
41930CB00041B/2650